Bodies of Water

# Lakes and Ponds

## Cassie Mayer

Heinemann Library
Chicago, Illinois

Customer Service 888-454-2279
Visit our website at www.heinemannraintree.com

Designed by Joanna Hinton-Malivoire
Photo research by Erica Martin
Printed and bound in China by South China Printing Co. Ltd.

12 11 10 09 08
10 9 8 7 6 5 4 3 2 1

ISBN-10: 1-4034-9365-0 (hc)
ISBN-10: 1-4034-9369-3 (pb)

**The Library of Congress has cataloged the first edition of this book as follows:**
Mayer, Cassie.
 Lakes and ponds / Cassie Mayer.
   p. cm. -- (Bodies of water)
 Includes bibliographical references and index.
 ISBN-13: 978-1-4034-9365-1 (hc)
 ISBN-13: 978-1-4034-9369-9 (pb)
 1. Lakes--Juvenile literature. 2. Ponds--Juvenile literature. I. Title.
 GB1603.8.M39 2008
 551.48'2--dc22
                                        2006034053

**Acknowledgements**
The publishers would like to thank the following for permission to reproduce photographs: Alamy pp. **11** (Brian Atkinson), **13** (Alfa Foto Agency), **19** (Che Garman), **20** (Pixonnet.com), **21** (BL Images Ltd), **23** (shallow pond: Brian Atkinson; freight ship: Pixonnet.com); Corbis pp. **4** (NASA), **8** (Theo Allofs), **10** (Bob Krist), **18** (Tom Grill); Getty Images pp. **6** (National Geographic/Michael S. Lewis), **7** (Stone/Russell Kaye/Sandra-Lee Phipps), **9** (LOOK/Florian Werner), **14** (Lonely Planet/Mark Newman), **15** (Digital Vision), **16** (National Geographic/George Grall), **17** (John Bracegirdle), **23** (lake in a valley: Digital Vision); Jupiter Images p. **5** (Brand X Pictures/Don Mason).

Cover photograph reproduced with permission of Corbis (Zefa/Serge Kozak). Back cover photograph reproduced with permission of Getty Images (LOOK/Florian Werner).

Every effort has been made to contact copyright holders of any material reproduced in this book. Any omissions will be rectified in subsequent printings if notice is given to the publishers.

# Contents

# Lakes

water

Most of the Earth is covered by water.

Some of this water is in lakes.

A lake is a large area covered by water.

Most lakes have fresh water.
The water is not salty.

Lakes have land on all sides.

Lakes are smaller than oceans.

# Ponds

pond

A pond is a very small lake.

Ponds are shallow.

# How Lakes Form

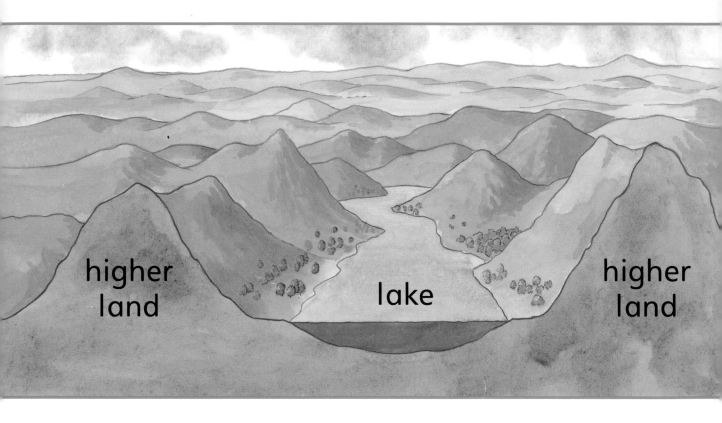

higher land

lake

higher land

Lakes form in low areas of the land.
The land around the lake is higher.

The low land fills with water.
The low land becomes a lake.

Some lakes are near mountains.

valley

Some lakes are in valleys.

# Lake Life

turtle

Lakes can have many animals.

Lakes can have many plants.

# How We Use Lakes

People use lakes for drinking water.

People use pipes to bring lake
water to them.

People use lakes to move goods.

People use lakes to reach new places.

# Lake Facts

Lake Baikal is the largest lake in the world. It is in Russia.

Lake Superior is the second largest lake in the world. It is in the United States and Canada.

# Picture Glossary

 **goods**  things that people buy and sell

 **shallow**  does not go down far; not deep

 **valley**  a low area of land. Valleys are between mountains or hills.

# Index

**Note to Parents and Teachers**
This series introduces bodies of water and their unique characteristics. Discuss with children bodies of water they are already familiar with, such as ones that exist in the area in which they live. Use page 12 to introduce how diagrams can be used as learning tools. Ask students to compare the type of information conveyed in a diagram to the information communicated in photographs.

The text has been chosen with the advice of a literacy expert to enable beginning readers success in reading independently or with moderate support. An expert in the field of geography was consulted to ensure accurate content. You can support children's nonfiction literacy skills by helping them use the table of contents, headings, picture glossary, and index.